HEROES of AMERICA ★ ILL

Benjamin Franklin

BY JACK KELLY

Illustrations by Ortiz Tafalla

4277

BARONET BOOKS, New York, New York

HEROES OF AMERICA™

Edited by
Joshua Hanft and Rochelle Larkin

HEROES OF AMERICA™ is a series of dramatized lives of great Americans especially written for younger readers. We have selected men and women whose accomplishments and achievements can inspire children to set high goals for themselves and work with all of us for a better tomorrow.

Table of Contents

Chapter   **Page**

1. A Hard Lesson.....................   5
2. Making Plans.......................   14
3. Finding a Trade   23
4. Apprenticeship   32
5. The Power of Print.................   41
6. On His Own   52
7. Philadelphia Days   61
8. On to England.....................   77
9. Citizen Franklin   88
10. *Poor Richard's Almanac* 100
11. Lightning Strikes 116
12. Ben at War 130
13. Life in London 146
14. Leadership........................ 163
15. America's Struggle Starts........... 176
16. From Colonies to Nation 190
17. Mission to France 206
18. Working for Peace 221
19. Ben Franklin, American 232

Important Dates

1706   Benjamin Franklin born in Boston

1718   Ben becomes a printer's apprentice

1723   Ben runs away to Philadelphia

1727   Ben starts his own printing shop

1730   Ben and Deborah Read marry

1733   *Poor Richard's Almanac* is first published

1748   Ben retires from the printing business

1752   Ben's experiments with electricity

1757   Ben goes to England for a long stay

1776   Ben helps write the Declaration of Independence

1783   Ben negociates treaty to end the Revolutionary War

1787   Ben helps write the Constitution

1790   Benjamin Franklin dies in Philadelphia

Chapter 1

A Hard Lesson

If you lived in Boston in the early 1700s, you couldn't get away from water. The city was surrounded by water. On one side was the harbor that led to the Atlantic Ocean, on the other the Charles River. There were plenty of lakes, ponds and marshes all around.

One day, in one of those marshes, a group of boys was splashing in the water trying to net fish.

"I've caught one!" a boy cried out. A silvery fish flopped and wiggled in his net.

"See Those Rocks?"

BEN FRANKLIN

"We could catch a lot more fish if this water weren't so muddy," one of the boys said.

"I have an idea," another declared.

"Oh, Ben Franklin has another idea." His friends laughed. "Another big idea."

"Don't my ideas make sense?" Ben said. "Remember those swimming paddles I invented? Whoever used them could swim faster than anybody."

The boys had to admit that Ben usually knew what he was talking about. Sometimes he seemed as smart as a grown-up—or even smarter.

"So what's your idea?" one of his friends asked.

"See those rocks?" Ben said, pointing to a big pile. "They're nice and square. If we pile them along the bottom of the salt marsh, pretty soon we'll have a wharf we can walk on. Then we can get to where the fish are without getting our feet wet."

"Let's do it!"

"But wait," one cautious boy said. "Some workmen left those stones there. They're going to build a house with them."

"But *we* need them for our wharf," Ben told him. "Now let's get to work." Ben couldn't resist any kind of project or adventure like this. It was fun to build things and see how they turned out.

By piling the stones up, they soon had a dry place to stand. Now they could walk farther out and place more stones.

It was a hot day. The work soon had them sweating. The boys weren't very big, and some of the blocks were so heavy, it took three boys to carry them. Ben was taller than the rest. He grunted as he picked up stones by himself.

By evening they'd made a solid wharf way out into the marsh. It would be a perfect fishing spot.

"That really was a good idea, Ben," one of his friends said.

"Let's Get to Work."

BEN FRANKLIN

It was already getting dark, so it was too late to fish. The boys headed for home, tired but proud of all the work they'd done. None of them gave any thought to what would happen when the workmen returned in the morning to find their stones missing.

Ben's family lived in a four-room house with a single fireplace for heat. He had many brothers and sisters—sometimes thirteen children at once gathered at the table. The house had only one window and not much furniture.

Yet the Franklin family was a happy one. The food Ben's mother cooked was plain, but there was always plenty of it. They ate bread or cornmeal mush with milk for breakfast. Dinner was usually a meat stew with vegetables and potatoes. They had no forks and very few knives.

That night after dinner, some friends of Ben's parents dropped by to discuss the events of the day. Even though he was a boy, Ben liked to listen to the adults talk. He was interested in everything that went on around him. He knew that people respected his father, whose name was Josiah, as someone who could give them good advice.

Soon it was time for bed. After all his efforts building the wharf, Ben fell asleep quickly.

"Ben, come in here."

Ben could tell from his father's voice the next day that he wasn't happy. Ben went into the front room. His father was standing there with a workman.

"This man says he had some stones ready to build a house down by the marsh. Someone took them. He was told that you and your friends may have done it."

"Yes, father. We needed those stones for a wharf."

"A wharf?"

Ben explained their plan. He knew it wasn't

"Nothing Is Useful That's Not Honest."

really right for them to take someone else's stones. But he told his father how practical it was, how it made it so much easier to catch fish. His father listened carefully. He was serious, but he wasn't angry.

"You always told me to do things that were useful," Ben explained. "That wharf is very useful."

"It's true, Ben," his father said. "Usefulness is good. But those stones did not belong to you. Nothing is truly useful that's not honest."

Ben understood. He and his friends had to go to the salt marsh and put the stones back. They hated to take their fishing spot apart, and pulling all the stones out of the water was even harder than it had been to build the wharf in the first place!

By the time he'd lugged the last stone back to the pile, Ben had learned a valuable lesson. From now on, he always would try to deal honestly with everyone. Any other way of doing things just wasn't worth it.

Chapter 2

Making Plans

"I want to be a sailor," Ben Franklin told his father. Ben was eight years old and he was sure he knew what he wanted to be when he grew up.

What could be more fun than to go to sea on one of the big sailing ships that were always docked at Boston's waterfront? The ships brought molasses from the West Indies, spices, cotton, and big barrels of wine. Sometimes they brought slaves from Africa. They sailed away with salted codfish and animal hides and lumber.

What Could Be More Fun than Going to Sea?

BEN FRANKLIN

"Where have you come from?" Ben asked the sailors who swaggered around Boston's streets.

They told about the strange places they'd seen. They told about fighting off pirates out on the ocean, who tried to hold up their ships and steal their cargo.

In those days, the east coast of America was settled with colonies owned by England and ruled by the king. If you wanted to go somewhere, it was easiest to go by water. Most of the roads were only muddy trails. Almost everyone lived near the coast. Farther inland, the deep forests held wild animals and the lands of Native Americans, whom the settlers called Indians.

Ben always loved to hear his father tell the story of when he had sailed across the ocean. Like many people in the colonies, Josiah was born and raised in the Old World. The men of Josiah's family were blacksmiths in England. After he married and had a few children, he decided to see what life was like in America.

"Storms threw our little ship around like it was a toy," Josiah would tell his son. "Big green waves loomed higher than the ship's masts. Sometimes we wondered if we would ever reach America."

In England, Josiah had learned the trade of dying clothes. But when he arrived in Boston he found that few people wanted colorful clothes. Most of the residents, like Josiah himself, were Puritans. They believed in plain gray clothing and a simple life.

But everybody needed candles for light, and soap to wash with, so Josiah went into the business of making these.

After a few years Josiah's wife died. Many people died young in those days. The doctors of the day didn't know how to cure dreaded diseases like smallpox. Several of Josiah's children also died.

Everyone Spent Time Reading.

BEN FRANKLIN

Josiah married another woman. Her name was Abiah. They had more children, until there were a total of seventeen altogether.

When Benjamin Franklin was born, on January 17, 1706 in Boston, his family was living on Milk Street near the Old South Church. Because he was born on Sunday, he was taken across the street and baptized that same day. Ben was the youngest boy in the family. Two sisters followed him.

Everyone in Ben's family spent time reading. Books were among the most treasured possessions in the Franklin household. Ben learned to read when he was very young. He couldn't ever remember not being able to read. He read many of his father's books, even though they were mostly on religious subjects and not very entertaining.

Ben liked the books of poetry better. He tried writing some poems of his own when he was about seven.

BEN FRANKLIN

Sometimes Ben went to his father's shop to watch him making candles and soap. His father didn't have much time to spend talking to Ben. He had many orders to fill. If people didn't get their candles, their houses would be dark.

Ben didn't think his father's trade was very exciting.

It will be a lot more fun to be a sailor and fight pirates than to work in a stuffy candle shop, he thought.

Ben's father didn't think that a sailor's life was a good one. He wanted something different for his youngest son. One evening they talked about it.

"You're a smart boy, Ben," his father said. "You have the makings of a scholar. I think it would be good if you were to become a minister of the church. We are told to give a tenth of our goods to the church, and you are my tenth son. So next week you will start your education at the Boston Grammar

Watching Him Make Candles and Soap

School."

Children in early America didn't always go to school. Parents would teach them to read and write at home. They would usually go to work by the time they were eight or nine. Life was hard, and even children had to pitch in and help. It was a special privilege to receive a formal education at school.

At eight years of age, Ben wasn't sure how he'd like being a minister all his life. He still thought that the life of a sailor sounded a lot more exciting.

Soon, though, he began to look forward to going to school. It would be an adventure to learn all the things they would teach him there. He was proud that his father thought he was smart enough to become a scholar.

Chapter 3

Finding a Trade

Ben started attending classes at the Boston Grammar School right away. The plan was for him to study there for six years, learning Latin and Greek and religion and philosophy. Afterward, he would go to Harvard College for four more years.

When I graduate I'll be a minister, Ben thought. *I wonder what it will be like?*

It was hard for him to know just what he wanted at that age. He knew, at least, that ministers spent a lot of time with books, and Ben loved to

He Became the Best Student.

read about almost any subject.

Ben was smart. He quickly became the best student in his class. His teachers were impressed that this son of a simple candlemaker had read so many books and that he learned his lessons so easily.

"Benjamin, you've done enough work to move up to the next class," his teacher told him in the middle of the year. "And if you keep studying hard, you can advance yet another level before the year is over."

But Josiah Franklin had begun to rethink his decision. Ben had a practical mind. He was a curious and questioning boy. This meant he was really more suited to take up a worldly profession than to be a minister. A minister had to be pious; he had to take religion very seriously.

"Ben, we've decided to take you out of the grammar school," Josiah told his son at the end of the year. "We're going to send you to Mr. Brownell's school instead. He will prepare you for whatever trade you choose."

Mr. Brownell taught reading and arithmetic to boys and girls in a little school two blocks from Ben's house. Mr. Brownell was a gentle teacher who encouraged Ben in his reading and writing. When the end of the year came, Ben had done well in every subject except arithmetic, which he failed.

Ben's parents decided he had learned enough. A family couldn't make ends meet unless everybody worked, so after only two years of school, Ben went to work in his father's shop.

Benjamin Franklin would grow up to become a very educated man—a scientist and a statesman. Almost everything he knew, he learned on his own. Though he never attended school again after those two years, he continued to read and study all his life.

For two years he worked beside his father in

After Only Two Years of School

the candle shop. Josiah knew that Ben wasn't happy. He felt it was important for a boy to find a trade that suited him. He was afraid that if Ben didn't find something he liked soon, he would run off and become a sailor.

Occasionally, when they had a little time, Ben and his father would walk through Boston to talk with some of the other tradesmen. "It's important to learn a good craft," his father would tell him. "Then you'll always be able to support yourself."

One good thing about living in the colonies was that a boy had a choice of the job he wanted to take up. In England it was harder to move into a new trade. Most boys went into the same trade their fathers had followed.

Ben still couldn't make up his mind about a trade. "He's always got a book in his hands," his mother suggested. "Maybe he should try being a printer. Then he could make books."

BEN FRANKLIN

Ben's brother James had come back from England a year earlier. Over there, he'd learned to be a printer and had bought a printing press. James was nine years older than Ben. He now had a printing shop in Boston.

Ben was fascinated by the way books were printed. Little blocks with raised backward letters had to be lined up by hand, one by one, line by line, in a frame. Then ink was applied and the printing press pushed paper against the letters, called type. "I think I'd like to work as a printer," Ben told his father.

This was an important decision. Ben was twelve years old. He had to agree to work for his brother until he was twenty-one. He would receive no pay, only his room and board. In return, Ben's brother would teach him what he needed to know to become a printer.

When he walked into his brother's shop that

Starting His Life's Work

first day, Ben knew that he was starting on what probably would be his life's work. Though he would do many other things in his long life, Ben Franklin always thought of himself as a printer first.

Chapter 4

Apprenticing

Apprentices in Ben Franklin's day had to obey their masters at all times. In return, the master provided them with food, clothes and a place to sleep. He taught them everything they needed to know about the craft so they could one day become master craftsmen themselves.

But apprentices were still boys. They often played tricks on their masters, or got into mischief. If they didn't break the rules, they were always seeing how far they could bend them.

Apprentices Were Still Boys.

Ben was no exception. He did little things that annoyed James. Because they were brothers, Ben expected to be treated better than just any apprentice. But James was strict with his brother. Sometimes he even hit him to make him obey.

Like all apprentices, Ben wore a leather apron and white shirt. He had little time for play. Besides his work setting type and helping to run the press, Ben had to get to the shop at six in the morning to start the fire and fetch water. He swept the floor and made sure the place was clean. He ran errands for his brother and waited on customers who came into the shop. It was a lot of work for a twelve-year-old boy.

But Ben still found time to read. He was able to borrow books from some of the men who came around the print shop. He read early in the morning and at lunchtime. He would finish the books at night by candlelight and give them back in the morning.

BEN FRANKLIN

One of the books he read described the benefits of not eating meat. Ben decided he would try a vegetarian diet. At the time, he and James were both staying in a house near the shop. James paid for their room and meals.

"Instead of paying for my meals," Ben suggested to his brother, "why not give me half the money you're spending now, and I'll buy my own food."

James was happy to save money this way. The people they roomed with thought Ben was odd to eat only vegetables, but Ben didn't care. Because bread and potatoes and vegetables were cheap, Ben was able to buy his food for very little. The money James gave him was twice what he needed. He saved the rest to buy more books.

When his brother and the other men from the printing shop went to lunch, Ben stayed behind. He ate a light meal of bread, a few raisins and a glass

Ben Said Girls Could Learn as Well as Boys.

of water and spent the rest of the time on his studies.

Ben had a friend named John Collins who also liked to read. The two boys would often pick some subject that was being talked about in Boston and discuss it, each trying to prove his point. For example, once Ben argued that girls could learn as well as boys and should be given the chance to go to school.

Ben learned from these discussions that it's not a good idea to contradict someone outright. A better way to win an argument is to agree with the person as much as you can, but draw him into seeing your point of view.

When they were going to be too busy to see each other, the boys carried on their discussion by sending letters to each other. Ben showed some of these letters to his father.

"Your spelling and punctuation are certainly

better than John's," his father said. "But I'm afraid he has a better way of expressing his ideas. You don't pay much attention to the way you say things."

Ben realized that his father was right. Being able to write well was an important skill. He began to read articles from old magazines that he thought were well written. He began to write his own versions of the articles. After a lot of practice, Ben sometimes was able to produce writing that was better than the original. That gave him confidence that someday he could be an important writer.

Ben was a quick learner. After a few years in the shop, he knew all the aspects of printing. But he was becoming restless. He did not like having to do what his brother told him.

One morning, James announced that he was going to start a new venture.

"I'm going to publish a newspaper," he told Ben. "It'll be the most interesting paper in the colonies

"I'm Going to Publish a Newspaper."

and everyone will be talking about it."

Some people thought James was foolish. There were already two papers in Boston. Because they were closely tied to the government, they never printed anything controversial.

"Those other papers are boring," James declared. "My paper will drive Demon Dullness from Beacon Hill."

Ben couldn't wait to help with this exciting new project.

Chapter 5

The Power of Print

James started his newspaper in 1720, when Ben was fourteen. He called it *The New England Courant*. It came out once a week. It wasn't like newspapers are today, but was printed on both sides of a single small sheet of paper.

James made his paper more lively by printing essays that made fun of the government or the religious authorities of Boston. He and his friends would write the pieces and sign them with funny made-up names like "Abigail Afterwit" or "Ichabod

People Were Eager to Get Each Issue.

Henroost."

James sent his young apprentice into the streets to sell the paper. Ben saw how eager people were to get each issue, how they laughed or argued about the things they read.

I could write something just as good for the paper, he thought to himself. *But James would never print it. He thinks of me just as his little brother and his apprentice.*

Ben thought of a way to have his own writing printed in the paper. He wrote a letter in a hand-writing that didn't look like his, and signed it "Silence Dogood." Then he slipped it under the door of the shop at night.

The next day, while he did his chores around the shop, he listened as his brother read the letter to the other men who wrote for the paper. They all thought this "Silence Dogood" was a witty person and wondered who could be writing under that name. The next Monday, when the *Courant* came out, Ben's "Dogood" letter was included. Ben was very pleased.

Over the next six months, Ben wrote fourteen more letters in the name of the young widow, "Silence Dogood." He made fun of hoop skirts, which were in fashion in Boston. He joked about people who got drunk but used another word for it, like "mellow," or "feverish." He wrote against religious bigotry and in favor of freedom of speech and education for women.

After a while, Ben could think of nothing more to write, so he stopped sending the "Dogood" letters to the paper. Someone guessed that Ben had been the one writing the letters. Ben admitted it. The men who hung around the paper laughed and told Ben he was a good writer. But James resented his brother for playing such a trick.

It wasn't long before James got into trouble

Ben Wrote Fourteen More Letters.

himself. He published an article that made fun of the government for not cracking down on the pirates who were robbing Boston's ships.

The city officials said he'd gone too far. He had insulted the government, and that wasn't allowed. They threw James into jail for a month.

Ben continued to put out the *Courant* while James sat in jail. He thought it was unjust to jail a man for saying what he thought.

All the controversy made even more people want to read the *Courant*. When he was released, James continued to write witty articles about the government and the town's religious leaders. A few months later, the city council ruled that James could no longer publish the *Courant*.

"What am I going to do?" James asked his friends.

"I have an idea," one of them said. "Make your brother Ben the publisher."

To do this, James had to release Ben from his contract as apprentice. He still made Ben promise secretly to work the years that remained till he turned twenty-one.

Ben was now seventeen. At six feet, he was taller than most grown men. He was strong from hard work, healthy from his vegetable diet. He knew as much about printing as his brother, and he could put out the newspaper on his own, but he didn't think it was right that he should still have to sweep and haul water and do all the other menial chores of an apprentice.

He and James began to argue more and more. Ben didn't always do what he was told. He talked back to his brother when he thought he was right. They took their dispute to their father. Ben argued that James was unfair to him.

"He treats me like his servant," Ben complained. "I think he should be kinder to me, his own

"I Expect You to Do as You're Told."

brother."

"You're my brother, but you're also my apprentice," James said. "I expect you to do as you're told."

"You released me as your apprentice," Ben said.

"That was only on paper."

"Ben, your brother's right," Ben's father told him. "He's taught you to be a good printer. You owe him your labor until your term is up. But James, you have to learn to keep your temper."

The brothers tried to work together, but Ben kept getting on his brother's nerves. They argued almost every day. Ben decided that he would be better off working for a different printer.

When James heard that Ben was thinking of looking for another job, he went to all the other printers in Boston and asked them not to hire his brother. They agreed. It was actually a crime for an apprentice to run away from his master before his time was up.

Ben began to think of moving on. He loved Boston, but he had made enemies there. Some people thought it was wrong for a boy his age to be critical of such learned men as Cotton Mather, a well-known clergyman and scholar, or the colony's governor.

Ben took some of his books down to a bookseller's shop and sold them. He was sorry to do so, but he needed the money.

Next he arranged with his friend John Collins to get him a ticket on a ship that was bound for New York. He didn't want anybody to know he was leaving. He packed his things in a trunk and got on the ship just before it pulled out.

A short time after he left, an advertisement ran in the *Courant*. It said, "James Franklin, printer, wants likely lad for apprentice."

At seventeen, Ben said good-bye to Boston. He was off to seek his fortune in a new city.

He Had Made Enemies.

Chapter 6

On His Own

Finally I'm on the sea! Ben thought as the sailing sloop swept down the coast toward New York. All through his youth he had dreamed of sailing the world's oceans. There was nothing to stop him from becoming a sailor now if he wanted to, but he had lost interest in going to sea as a profession. The printing trade was what he knew and loved.

New York was a bustling town at the southern end of the island of Manhattan. Carts and wagons full of goods clattered through the busy streets.

Everybody seemed to be in a hurry.

As he walked into a print shop, Ben smelled the familiar odor of fresh ink.

"I'm looking for Mr. William Bradford," he announced.

"That's me," said a man with gray hair and a kindly face.

Ben told the man his name and that he was an experienced printer. "I thought you might have a job for me."

"I wish I did," Mr. Bradford said. "But the printing business is slow in this town."

Mr. Bradford was a little suspicious about this teenager at first. But as they chatted, he realized that Ben really did know a lot about printing. They talked for a long time and became friends.

"I would like to send you to another printer, but I'm the only one in New York," Bradford said. "However, my son runs a print shop in Philadelphia. I

Ben Set Out for Philadelphia.

know he's been looking to replace a helper who died recently. You could probably get a job with him."

Ben immediately set out for Philadelphia. He couldn't afford the stagecoach that connected the two cities, so he boarded a boat.

Philadelphia was the capital of Pennsylvania. It was a colony that had been given by the king to a man named William Penn. Forty years before Ben arrived there, Penn had come over from England with a group of Quakers. Like the Puritans, the Quakers were a religious group who believed in plain living. But unlike the Puritans, they tolerated other religions.

William Penn made friends with the Native Americans in his vast tract of land. He established Philadelphia, which in the Greek language means "city of brotherly love." By the time Ben arrived in 1723, Philadelphia was a commercial center even bigger than Boston.

BEN FRANKLIN

The streets were quiet that Sunday morning. But Ben had only one thing on his mind. He was hungry!

Most of the shops were closed because the people were in church. Ben saw a boy walking along the street eating a loaf of bread. He asked where he could find the bakery. When he went there, he discovered that people in Pennsylvania made a different kind of bread than he was used to in Boston. And it was cheap. He was able to buy three big loaves.

The sun was shining, and Ben went walking along the street eating his loaf of fresh bread and carrying the other two under his arms. He was dressed in his leather working clothes, some extra underwear stuffed into his pockets. He looked ragged and tired from his journey.

He heard someone laugh. It was a girl about his own age. She was sweeping her steps and couldn't

Walking Along the Street

help giggling when she saw the young man walking by, his mouth stuffed with bread.

She smiled at Ben, waved, then shyly looked away.

There are some pretty girls in Philadelphia, Ben thought.

He went back to the wharf and gave the rest of his bread to a woman and her child who had come down the river with him. The next place he stopped was a Quaker meeting house, where members held their religious services. Ben slipped into a pew and before too long, he fell asleep. No one bothered him. When the service was over, the Quakers gently woke him.

"Where could I get a place to stay?" Ben asked a friendly looking young man.

"If thou will walk with me, I'll show thee a good place," the man said. That was the way the Quakers chose to speak.

BEN FRANKLIN

Ben took a room in an inn and slept all day. He got up to eat supper, then slept all night, too.

The next morning, Ben paid his bill with his last Dutch dollar. He headed out into the city with no money, and not knowing a soul. He had no idea what awaited him.

He Desperately Needed a Job.

Chapter 7

Philadelphia Days

"Can you direct me to Andrew Bradford's printing shop?" Ben asked a man on a Philadelphia street. A few minutes later Ben entered the shop, hoping to obtain the job he desperately needed.

"When I met your father in New York, he told me you were looking for a helper in your shop. I think I could fill the position very well."

"I'm sorry," the printer told him, "I've already hired someone."

Ben was downhearted. He had to find some

kind of work if he was to eat.

Fortunately, the younger Mr. Bradford was also very friendly. He took Ben to his house for breakfast, and offered him a place to stay for as long as he needed it. His father, William, had just come down from New York by stagecoach. The two men talked about what was best for Ben to do.

"There's that new printer, Samuel Keimer," Andrew said. "He might want an assistant who knows printing."

William Bradford took Ben around to Keimer's shop. Keimer didn't have much business. He was setting the type for a poem he'd written himself. But he agreed to let Ben help out for a few hours a day. If Ben proved useful, Keimer would hire him full-time.

So Ben went to work at what he loved. The press in Keimer's shop was an old one and not in good shape. Ben did what he could to fix it. He soon

What Was Best for Ben

learned that Keimer knew nothing about printing. He could arrange the letters in their frame well enough, but he was at a loss when it came to working the press.

Ben soon took over all the skilled labor in the shop and became Mr. Keimer's right hand man.

"You shouldn't be boarding with the Bradfords," his employer told him. "They're my competitors. I'll arrange for another room for you."

By this time, Ben's chest full of clothes, which he'd sent down from New York, had arrived. He went to the wharf with a wheelbarrow to pick it up. He wheeled it up the street to the Read household, where Keimer told him he was to stay.

When he arrived he was quite surprised. The door was opened for him by the same girl who had laughed at him his first morning in Philadelphia.

"We've seen each other before," he said. "I'm Ben Franklin."

"I'm Deborah Read," the girl said. "Very pleased to meet you."

Ben hefted his sea chest up the stairs to the attic room that Deborah pointed out to him.

How lucky to get to know someone my own age right away, Ben thought. He liked Deborah, but he hardly imagined what would happen later—that this was the woman he would marry.

Ben soon realized that he was the most skilled printer in town. Mr. Keimer was an odd fellow who was only a beginner at the trade. Andrew Bradford had experience, but could hardly read and had nothing like Ben's background with books.

Ben worked as hard as always and saved his money. He had been living in Philadelphia for about six months when he received a letter from his brother-in-law, who was a sea captain. He wrote to urge Ben to return home. Ben's parents didn't know where he'd gone and were worried. If Ben would go

"The Governor of Pennsylvania!"

back, they would welcome him and forgive him for running away.

I've gone through too much to earn my freedom, Ben thought. *I'm earning my own way, and I have no desire to go back and let James lord it over me again. Besides, I like Philadelphia.*

He wrote his brother-in-law a long letter explaining why he wouldn't return.

One day Ben and Mr. Keimer were working in the back of the shop when a man came in. Keimer grabbed Ben by the sleeve and whispered to him, "Do you know who that is? It's Sir William Keith, the governor of Pennsylvania! He's come to see me, probably to give me some business printing government documents. What luck!"

They both went to the front of the shop.

"I'm looking for a young man named Benjamin Franklin," the governor said. "I was told he worked here."

Mr. Keimer's mouth dropped open. He felt very envious as the governor took Ben by the arm and led him out of the shop. "Your brother-in-law showed me the letter you sent him," the governor told Ben as they strolled along the street. "There are few men in Pennsylvania who can write as well as you."

Ben glowed with the praise. It was quite a compliment for someone with only two years of school!

Governor Keith took Ben to a tavern. He had a proposition for him.

"We need a really good printing house here in Philadelphia. It will help me to communicate with all the people of Pennsylvania. I want you to set one up. I'll help you get started by giving you a lot of the official government business. What do you think of that?"

Ben could hardly believe it. Barely eighteen, owner of his own business, and friends with the governor! It didn't take him long to say yes.

The Governor Took Ben by the Arm.

BEN FRANKLIN

Keith suggested that Ben return to his father to get the money to start the shop. He gave him a letter explaining that Ben had the governor's full backing and support.

Before he left for Boston, Ben went for dinner at Governor Keith's elegant house. He bought a new suit and a watch with his savings. Only seven months after he'd left home, he was on a ship bound for Boston.

It felt fine to return home. There was his father's shop. There was his mother, who welcomed him with a big hug. Everybody was glad to see him. Almost everybody.

Ben went down to James's print shop to say hello to his brother and the others he had worked with. James was not friendly. Ben made matters worse by showing off his new watch and giving the workers some coins to buy drinks. James felt insulted and swore he would never forgive his brother. It was not until many years later that they made up.

"Isn't this a grand opportunity?" Ben eagerly asked his father after he'd explained Governor Keith's offer.

Ben's father read the governor's letter carefully. "I don't know that it is, Ben," he said. "I don't think it's a wise idea to give a young man such responsibility. If you wait a few years and save your money, when you reach twenty-one, I'll help you to get started, as I did James. Right now you're just too young."

His father advised Ben to go back to Philadelphia and work hard. "Behave respectfully and make the people there think well of you. Don't joke and mock people the way you did here. It will hurt your reputation."

Though he was disappointed not to have the money for his printing shop, Ben was glad to leave

They Became Close Friends.

Boston with his father's blessing this time. The Reads were glad when Ben returned. Deborah's father had died suddenly. Ben was now able to help them out with some of the chores around the house. Deborah introduced him to other young people she knew. They played music together and became close friends.

Ben reported to Governor Keith what his father had said.

"That's all right," the governor replied. "I'll back you in the shop myself. I want you to book a passage to London right away. I'll give you letters of credit that will be honored there. You'll have enough to buy a fine printing press and whatever else you need to go into business."

Ben was excited. He had always wanted to visit London, a city far bigger than any town in the colonies. Now the dream of having his own shop looked like it would come true, too.

He had to wait several months before the next ship left for London—there was only one per year. While he waited, he made a list of all the virtues he wanted to follow in his life—to be thrifty, hard-working, humble, loyal. He decided to record in a notebook his progress toward achieving these traits. He kept the notebook for many years afterward, checking off how he was doing with each virtue.

He and Deborah Read saw a lot of each other. They began to talk of marriage. Debby's mother knew that Ben was planning a trip to London. Because they were both only eighteen, she advised them to wait until Ben returned. They agreed to do so.

His ship sailed in November of 1724. He went to see the governor to get the letters of credit that would allow him to buy the equipment he needed. The governor's assistant said Sir William was too busy.

His Ship Sailed in November.

"The letters will be delivered to the ship's captain," he said. "He'll give them to you in London."

Ben boarded the ship. They cruised down the Delaware Bay and turned east. Ben stood at the ship's bow looking out into the Atlantic Ocean. He was ready for a new adventure.

Chapter 8

On to England

Sailing to London with Ben was his friend James Ralph. The two young men were lucky; a rich man had canceled his voyage, so they were allowed a decent cabin even though they had paid only for bunks below deck.

No sea voyage was easy in those days. The ships were small, with sails, relying on the wind to move them. It took six weeks or more to cross the Atlantic Ocean. That November they encountered one storm after another. Everyone was glad finally

"I See Nothing with Your Name on it."

to arrive in England.

"I believe you have some letters for me," Ben told the captain.

"No, I see nothing with your name on it, Mr. Franklin."

"From Governor Keith," Ben said. "I'm sure they must be there."

"Look in the mailbag yourself," the captain said.

Ben was shocked to find that the governor had sent him no letters of credit, no introductions, nothing.

Ben had made friends on the crossing with an older man, a Quaker named Thomas Denham. Mr. Denham advised him now, "Don't expect letters of credit from Keith. He has no credit to give. He's simply not reliable, Ben. Everybody knows it."

"I didn't know it," Ben said. "I trusted him. What am I going to do now? I have very little money."

"You have a skill," Mr. Denham said. "That's even better. Go get a job as a printer. You'll learn things you can use when you get back to Philadelphia."

That's just what Ben did. He and James took a room together and Ben got a job with Palmer's, a respectable London printing company.

Both young men found London a fascinating place. It was far bigger than any city in America. They saw fancy aristocrats being driven in carriages and attended by servants in silk uniforms. At the same time they saw masses of poor people living in awful tenements and begging for food. There were ornate theaters and coffeehouses, and busy taverns that made Philadelphia seem tame by comparison. Ben was happy to find that there were many booksellers in town.

Now Ben became serious about saving money.

Both Young Men Found London Fascinating.

BEN FRANKLIN

He found a job that paid more—at Watts's printing house, one of the biggest in London. Fifty other men worked there.

Though Ben was an expert at setting type, he asked to help operate the presses because he missed the hard work. He showed the other workers how he could carry two heavy trays of lead type up and down stairs, one in each hand. Most of them had trouble carrying even one tray.

"He's certainly a strong one, he is," one of the men declared. "And I don't see how he does it, just drinking water all the time."

Ben was still eating his vegetable diet. The other workers drank beer with breakfast and all during the day. A boy ran over from the alehouse with glasses of beer for them while they worked. Ben thought they were foolish.

"You fellows spend half your money on beer and are never able to save anything. That just doesn't make sense to me."

He wasn't able to persuade them to try his diet. They called him the "Water-American," because he took plain water with all his meals.

Ben also cut out his trips to the theater and the coffeehouses. Because there were no libraries, he arranged with a second hand bookstore to allow him to rent their used books.

By this time, Ben didn't think about Debby too often. He had written her one letter during the time he was enjoying all the novelties of London. He told her wouldn't be coming back anytime soon.

Ben was promoted to top typesetter at the company. Because he worked so quickly, his boss assigned him the rush jobs and paid him a bonus. He was impressed that Ben was so smart that he could discuss the ideas of the authors whose books he was setting into type.

Ben published a leaflet of his own, discussing a

"I'll Teach You How to Be a Merchant."

philosophical question. Through it, he was noticed by several prominent people in London.

Ben occasionally went to visit Thomas Denham, the friend from Philadelphia whom he'd met on the ship coming over.

"You've been over here a year and a half, Ben," Denham said. "You should start to think about going home. I'm returning to Philadelphia soon myself. I could use a bright assistant to help me in my store. I can pay you fifty pounds a year, and you will make more on commissions. I'll teach you how to be a merchant."

Fifty pounds was less than he was earning at the printing house, but Ben thought it was an opportunity he couldn't pass up. It was hard to get rich as a printer. Successful merchants made a lot of money. Besides, he missed Philadelphia. He wanted to go back.

So in October, 1726, almost two years after he'd

left home, Ben and Mr. Denham both boarded ship. The sailors cast off the lines, hoisted the sails, and they set off on the long ocean journey that would take them back to the New World and Philadelphia.

Back to the New World

Chapter 9

Citizen Franklin

The Philadelphia Ben returned to wasn't the same place he had left. The town had grown noticeably in those two years.

Samuel Keimer, the man Ben had worked for, was much more prosperous now. The busy city was producing more work for printers.

Governor Keith had been replaced. Now he was just a private citizen. When he saw Ben on the street he passed by without saying anything. He was ashamed, Ben knew, of the trick he'd played on him.

I have my own reason to be ashamed, Ben thought. *I certainly didn't treat Debby very kindly.*

When Ben's letter arrived saying he wouldn't be back for a long while, Deborah Read's mother urged her to marry another man. Ben was sorry to hear, on his return, that her husband was a cruel man who had left her and run off to the West Indies. She sat around the house now, sunk in low spirits.

Thomas Denham set up a wholesale business on Water Street. He taught the twenty-year-old Ben everything about buying and selling shipments of goods and about bookkeeping. Mr. Denham was kind to Ben, and Ben thought of him as a father.

Their business was just beginning to prosper when both men became ill. Being young, Ben was able to recover. Denham died. Ben was sad to lose a friend. He also found himself without a job.

"I guess I'll have to fall back on the trade I know

Ben Did Everything.

well," Ben thought. He went and asked Keimer for a job. Keimer hired him as foreman in his shop.

Ben did everything. He molded new letters to replace broken type. He made ink. He created engravings by scratching lines into copper, to print pictures in books and pamphlets. He trained the men who worked for Keimer, showing them the latest printing techniques he had learned in London.

Once he was back at it, Ben realized that he loved the printing trade more than anything. "I would rather be a leather-apron man than a merchant," he told everyone. "Printers print words and words have power. They can make people laugh or cry. They are the only way to spread ideas."

One of the men who worked for Keimer was Hugh Meredith. Hugh's father agreed to put up the money so that Ben and Hugh could start their own printing business. Because Ben was such an expert printer, they knew the venture would succeed.

They ordered a printing press from England and soon set up a small shop. It was a great day for the young men when their first customer walked in the door.

Hugh knew little about printing. After a few years, Ben borrowed some money and bought Hugh's share of the business. Ben was only twenty-four and he finally had what he had dreamed of—his own printing business.

About that same time, in 1730, Ben and Deborah Read moved in together and she became his wife. They couldn't get married in a church because they weren't sure if her first husband was dead or alive. But they were happy together, and Debby was a great help in Ben's business.

Ben already had a son named William by another woman. Debby accepted William into their house. Soon they had another son, Frankie. Ben loved this boy dearly, but when Frankie was four, he

His Own Printing Business

came down with smallpox and died. Later, Ben and Debby had a daughter, Sarah, whom they called Sally.

Owning his own business didn't mean instant success for Ben. He had to work hard. He still ate bread and milk for breakfast. He and his family lived upstairs from the shop.

"I'm not going to start wearing fancy clothes and living like a rich man," he told Debby. "When people hire a printer they want someone who's simple and honest."

In addition to the print shop, Ben and Debby kept a store where they sold all kinds of things. People could buy paper there, along with ink and quill pens, maps and legal forms, tea and coffee. Customers could even pick up groceries, liquor, and lottery tickets. Debby's widowed mother prepared herbs and ointments for them to sell.

They also sold a type of iron stove that Ben had

invented. It burned wood inside of it, and heated better than a fireplace. Franklin stoves are still used in houses today.

Because of his love of books, Ben became a seller and publisher of books. He issued the first medical book in the colonies, and the first novel.

Ben soon began printing a newspaper—the *Pennsylvania Gazette*. He covered the local news: fires and accidents, thefts and murders, and outbreaks of disease. He wrote witty essays, much like the Dogood letters, but without mocking or offending anyone.

Working hard at the printing, and the newspaper, Ben began to make money. Before long, he was able to help some of his workers go into business for themselves. "I know how hard it is for a young man to get started in business," he told them. "I'm always willing to help someone who has the talent and is willing to work hard."

A Chance to Know Important People

BEN FRANKLIN

His partners traveled to New York, Connecticut and South Carolina to establish print shops. They would send part of the profits back to Ben, and when they had saved enough, Ben would allow them to buy out his interest and own their own shops.

Ben was appointed to the position of clerk of the Pennsylvania Assembly, which made the laws for the colony. It gave him a chance to meet the lawmakers and get to know important people. It was also good for business. His shop received contracts to print money, laws and all sorts of documents.

Later, Ben was appointed postmaster of Philadelphia. He ran the post office from his store. At first, people had to come in to pick up their mail. Later Ben began one of the first mail delivery services in America. The deliverers were called "penny postmen" because people would have to pay a penny to receive a letter. Being postmaster also allowed Ben to distribute the *Gazette* for free.

BEN FRANKLIN

All this time, Ben continued to read and study. He taught himself to read French, Spanish, and Italian. He picked up a little of the Latin that he never had time to learn at school.

By the time he was in his thirties, Ben had achieved almost everything he'd hoped for—a prosperous business, a loving wife, two children, and many friends. The runaway apprentice had made good. He was happy with his life. He had no idea of the many changes that lay ahead — for himself and for his country.

Almost Everything He'd Hoped For

Chapter 10

Poor Richard's Almanac

"The first meeting of the junto will come to order!" Ben called out. A junto is a group of people who meet to discuss their interests. The eleven other men settled down. They were meeting in the back room of a tavern in Philadelphia. The year was 1727.

"As you know," Ben continued, "we are here to discuss interesting issues and questions, to pass on to each other whatever useful information we can, and to lend a hand when there is need."

"And to have a good time!" one of the men called out. The others laughed.

Ben smiled. "Of course. We'll always have time for a glass of wine and some fun. We're not going to be like the old men in the merchants club—always deadly serious."

"We're all tradesmen here," one man, a shoemaker, noted. "We could call ourselves the Leather Apron Club."

Like Ben, the men in his club worked at different crafts. One was a surveyor, one a silversmith, one a glassworker. Like Ben, most had not had the opportunity to attend school for long. None had been to college. The junto gave them an opportunity to learn from each other and to expand their knowledge.

"Our goal should be to improve ourselves," Ben said. "For men of common sense like ourselves, it's the practical thing to do. We'll bring in questions

"Is One Form of Government Best?"

to discuss at our regular Friday meeting."

"What kinds of things shall we discuss?" one man asked.

"We should start with the important questions of the day. For example: Is one form of government best for all men?"

"Or: If the king tries to take away a man's rights, should he resist?" a member suggested.

"But we will also talk about practical matters," Ben said, "such as how to stop a chimney from smoking too much. And we'll look into scientific questions, too. We might find out why dew forms on the outside of a tank of cold water in summer—or why there are fossils of seashells in the mountains!"

Ben had always loved to talk and to explore the mysteries of the world around him. The junto gave him the chance to do that, and to make friends, and also to gather material that he could use in his newspaper.

The junto became very popular. Many others wanted to join, but Ben thought the group should stay small. He encouraged people to start their own juntos. Soon there were discussion clubs all over Philadelphia.

This period in history, the 1700s, would come to be known as the Enlightenment. Also called the Age of Reason, it was a time in which scientific knowledge expanded very rapidly both in Europe and America. People still believed in God, but religion began to play a less important role in daily life. People believed that doing good works and learning about nature was more important than listening to preachers. Superstition began to die out. Education came to be seen as very important for everyone, not just for scholars.

If it made sense for people to improve themselves, then it was also logical that they should try to improve the communities that they lived in. Ben

The Junto Became Very Popular.

BEN FRANKLIN

Franklin believed in community service. He used the junto to put into action some of the ideas he'd always had for making Philadelphia a better place. He never accepted money for his ideas, or even his inventions. He believed everyone should benefit from them equally.

To begin with, the streets of the city had never been paved. When it rained, people couldn't cross the street without wading through mud. When the mud dried out, there was a great deal of dust.

"If we can raise money to pave one street," Ben proposed to his fellow club members, "it will show people how fine it would be if all the streets were paved!"

They convinced the merchants and residents on a street near the marketplace to pay for the street to be paved with stone. They all contributed to pay a man to sweep the street and take away the trash. People who came to the marketplace were impressed by the change. They all wanted their streets paved. The idea spread through the city.

Later Ben presented a paper to the junto. "I've looked at the problem of fire," he explained. "Most houses have fireplaces for heat, and candles for light. Most houses are made of wood. What happens? Fires break out. In a city like ours, where houses are close together, fire spreads. Many people lose their homes."

"What can we do about it?" another member asked.

"I have a plan," Ben said.

Just as when he was a boy, Ben took the role of leader. His plan was to organize a group of men who would volunteer to rush to any house where a fire had broken out. Each would carry a leather bucket. A line of men would pass buckets of water from hand to hand to put out the fire.

Ben helped start the first volunteer fire depart-

Fire Departments Formed in Philadelphia.

ment in America. Soon fire departments formed all over Philadelphia. They began to buy ladders and pumper wagons. They met, like the junto, every week to discuss ways of preventing and putting out fires. Soon Philadelphia had become one of the safest cities in the world.

"All of us are happy to lend our books to each other," Ben said at another junto meeting. "Wouldn't it be a good idea for us, and anyone else who's interested, to form a lending library? We could each contribute some money, buy books, and have them available for anyone to borrow."

Fifty people signed up to be members of this library. In a few years many more had joined. This was the first lending library in America, soon to be copied in many other cities.

Ben's ideas didn't stop there. Philadelphia didn't have a real police force then. Citizens were supposed to volunteer to be on watch at night. But the system didn't work well. Ben helped organize a group of paid watchmen who would be responsible to keep order.

While he was busy with all these improvements, Ben started up a new venture in his printing business. Almost every home in the colonies at that time had two books: a Bible and an almanac. The almanac came out every year and contained information on the rising and setting of the sun and moon; the stars, the tides, and the weather. It informed people on everything from how to plant peas to making pickles. It also contained jokes, poems, songs, and ways to make home remedies.

Ben began publishing his own almanac in 1733. He wrote it all himself. In many cases, he took old sayings and rewrote them to make them livelier. He used a different name—a pen name, Richard Saunders—and called the book *Poor Richard's Almanac*.

Poor Richard became very popular. People

Poor Richard's Almanac

thought of Richard as a real character. They loved his wit and followed his advice. His was the voice of the New World—practical, funny and full of common sense.

Ben, through Poor Richard, became famous for his sayings: "God helps those who help themselves." "Early to bed, early to rise, makes a man healthy, wealthy and wise." "There are no gains without pains."

Poor Richard's Almanac came out every year for twenty-five years. It was the most popular book in America. Soon people in colonies from the Carolinas to Massachusetts knew the name Benjamin Franklin.

Ben also started several grammar schools in towns around Pennsylvania. He headed a committee that established schools for African Americans and Native Americans. Remembering how his own father had had trouble paying for Ben's schooling, he made sure that poor children were able to come to school for free.

Through all these years, Ben was a very busy man. He and Debby made enough money to live comfortably, though Ben was never one to waste money on silly luxuries.

Benjamin Franklin got out of bed at five every morning and prayed to Powerful Goodness, which was what he called God. He always asked himself, *What good shall I do today?*

He studied and read books until eight. He worked until six in the evening, with two hours off for lunch. After supper, he visited with friends and listened to music. Before he went to bed at ten, he always thought, *What good did I do today?*

Ben was forty-two now. Many people in those days didn't live to reach that age. He had done many good works and had made plenty of money from his businesses.

"I've Always Been Interested in Lightning."

"I think it's time for me to change direction," he told Debby. "I don't see any point in just accumulating more and more money. I would rather have it said of me, 'He lived usefully' than 'He died rich.' So I've decided to retire."

"What are you going to do now, Pappy?" Debby asked him.

"I've always been interested in things like lightning," Ben said.

"Lightning?"

"Yes. For one thing, I'm going to find out what lightning really is."

Chapter 11

Lightning Strikes

Ben had always been curious about the things he saw around him. *Why does salt dissolve in water?* he asked. *Why does the sea sometimes glow in the dark? Why do earthquakes occur?*

In those days, science did not yet have answers for questions like these. The world was full of mysteries that no one could yet explain. Scientists, who were called philosophers, or "lovers of knowledge," were mostly amateurs. Anybody who could read books and who was curious about the world could

Science Did Not Have Answers.

become a "scientist."

Once when he was in Boston visiting his family, Ben went to see a show put on by a man named Dr. Archibald Spencer. By rubbing glass and amber rods, this man was able to produce "electrical fire," sparks. He hung a boy off the floor by silk cords and made a spark jump from the boy's nose. Everyone was amazed.

Ben bought some of this apparatus, or equipment, from Spencer in order to try the experiments with sparks himself. His friend Collinson in England sent him a large glass rod for producing electricity. Ben began to use Leyden jars. These were glass jars lined with tin foil, that could hold electricity produced by rubbing. By connecting several jars together with metal wires, Ben was able to produce an even bigger spark. He called this a "battery."

"You had better be careful with those experiments," Debby told him. "If you think you can use that electrical fire to kill a chicken, you might accidentally kill yourself!"

"Don't worry, my dear. I know what I'm doing."

But because electricity was so new, Ben *didn't* always know what he was doing. One time he did attempt to kill a turkey, and a bolt of electricity went right through the top of his head. It set off a loud bang and knocked him unconscious to the floor.

"I felt a shock through my whole body," he said afterward. He knew he had been lucky not to be killed.

By reading everything that had been written about electricity, Ben came to know as much as anybody in the world about this mysterious new force. People knew that rubbing a glass rod with silk produced one kind of electricity, and rubbing an amber rod with wool produced an opposite type.

Ben decided that there was only one kind of

People Came to See His Experiments.

electricity, but that it had two different charges. He named these "positive" and "negative." He found that something with a positive charge attracted an object with a negative charge, but repelled anything that also had a positive charge. This was the beginning of the modern understanding of electricity.

Ben wrote letters about electric charges, batteries, and what he called conductors, such as glass or amber, to his friends in England. His letters were published. They became the most up-to-date book about electricity. People in Europe were amazed that someone from the forests of the New World could know so much, especially this man who was a mere printer.

People now came to Ben Franklin's house in Philadelphia to see him perform his electrical experiments. A scientist was almost like a magician in those days. He seemed to have special powers. But Ben always tried to explain to his visitors that what he was doing was harnessing natural forces. This was science, not magic.

In 1752 he decided it was time to investigate something that had always fascinated him. He had observed that the lightning that flashed from the sky during a thunderstorm looked like a giant version of the electrical sparks he produced with his apparatus, his glass and amber rods.

"I would like to try an experiment," he told his son William, who was 21 at the time. "I will try to draw the electricity out of a thundercloud. I want you to help me."

"How will we do it?" William asked.

"You'll see. But don't tell anyone. Some people might think we're crazy."

"Why is that, Father?"

"Because it's not often you see a grown man flying a child's kite, especially in a thunderstorm."

The next time a thunderstorm approached

"To Draw Electricity Out of a Thundercloud"

Philadelphia, Ben and William went out to a pasture. Ben had made a kite out of silk, one that would hold up better in the rain than a paper kite. William ran across the field to help launch it. Dark clouds moved in.

"We'll stand under this shed so we don't get wet when it starts to rain," Ben said. "Let's see what happens."

Ben tied a key to one end of the kite string. He used a silk ribbon, which he knew wouldn't conduct electricity, to insulate himself from the string. He and William waited for quite a while.

"Nothing's happening," William said.

"Let's be patient a while longer," his father advised.

Ben kept touching the key to see if electricity was coming down the string. Nothing happened. He was about ready to give up when he saw the fibers on the kite string stand up, a sign of electrical charge.

Ben touched his knuckles to the key and felt a strong jolt of electricity. "That's it!" he shouted to William. "Electricity is coming from the clouds!"

As the rain made the string wet, a lot of electricity flowed down. William touched a Leyden jar to the key and was able to collect the charge.

Ben Franklin became famous for his experiment with the kite, and legendary to this day. He was made a member of the Royal Society in England, the most important scientific society in the world.

"Still," he told his friends, "I haven't produced anything useful. To advance knowledge is good, but I like to see my work benefit people."

"Maybe someday electricity will benefit people," a friend said.

Ben then turned his attention to a practical problem: protecting buildings from being hit by

He Attached a Lightning Rod to His House.

lightning. At that time, people saw lightning as a punishment from God. When a storm approached, the only protection was to pray and to ring church bells.

Ben figured that a pointed copper rod placed on a house, with a wire attached to send or conduct the lightning into the ground, could make the lightning harmless. He attached a lightning rod to his own house. He urged others to make use of this protection. In *Poor Richard's Almanac*, he printed instructions so that anybody who wished to could make a rod.

"That's blasphemy, Ben Franklin," some preachers warned. "People should not protect themselves from God's wrath."

"Don't be silly," Ben challenged them. "Thunder is no more supernatural than rain or hail or sunshine—and people always protect themselves against those."

BEN FRANKLIN

Lightning rods were put up on houses and barns throughout America and Europe. They saved many buildings from lightning strikes and fires. Ben's reputation as "the man who tamed lightning" spread all over the world.

Electricity was only one of many scientific subjects that Ben Franklin investigated. He invented bifocal eyeglasses, with reading and distance lenses in the same pair of glasses. He used them himself for many years. He invented a new kind of streetlight and a musical instrument called the armonica, inspired by the piano-like glass harmonica. He even designed a bathtub and urged people to bathe regularly.

Ben loved to devote his time to his scientific experiments and to making useful inventions. But America was still a partly wild place. He was soon called to more urgent duties as violence broke out in the mountains to the west.

Ben Invented Bifocal Eyeglasses.

Chapter 12

Ben at War

In the 1750s, the American colonies were still just a strip of settlements along the East Coast. A hundred miles inland was the frontier: dense forests, uncharted mountains. Roads were just dirt pathways. The vast interior of the American continent was yet to be settled.

Anyone who moved away from the coast entered lands that belonged to Native American tribes. The ancestors of some of these people had been living in the same area for thousands of years.

BEN FRANKLIN

Their ways were different from those of the European settlers. They did not believe that any person could own the land. The land was there for everyone to use.

The settlers had other ideas. They wanted this new land for themselves. They thought of the Indians as savages, people of no worth.

Ben Franklin would soon be caught up in the conflicts between settlers and tribes. Once he had retired from his printing business, he began to participate in the politics of his city and state. He was elected to the Pennsylvania Assembly, where he served for many years.

In 1753 Ben was appointed deputy postmaster general of all the colonies. This was a prestigious position with a yearly income and the chance to travel up and down the colonies to inspect the postal service. Ben improved the delivery of letters—he increased sending the mail between New York and

The Six Nations of the Iroquois

BEN FRANKLIN

Philadelphia from once a week to three times a week. He appointed his son William to his old job as postmaster of Philadelphia.

That same year Ben traveled to the frontier to confer with Native Americans. He and his companions rode on horseback for four days into the forest. They met with representatives of the six nations of the Iroquois. These were a group of tribes that had organized together under a central government.

The white men brought blankets and coats, knives and guns. They listened to the Indians, as they called them, and heard complaints: too many traders, too many settlers.

Ben was wary of the Indians at first. He didn't understand their language or the way they lived. But as time went by, he came to see them as dignified people who were being treated disrespectfully. Ben believed that all white people should deal with these Native Americans fairly, and stick to the treaties that were signed.

He saw how the Iroquois tribes were able to put differences aside and plan together. It might, he thought, be a lesson to the colonies, which still had no unified government.

Back in Philadelphia, Ben had his hands full. The Assembly was having continual problems with the Penn brothers in England, who actually owned Pennsylvania. Their father, William Penn, had been given this huge tract of land by the king of England years before. But when he died, the two brothers were only interested in profit. They refused to pay taxes on their holdings—Pennsylvania itself—but benefited from the work the colonists did there. Ben was a leader in trying to pressure the Penns to cooperate.

One morning in 1754, a man burst into Ben's home. "Ben, have you heard the news?" the man said breathlessly. "The French are coming. They've

Ben Had His Hands Full.

moved into western Pennsylvania."

"Isn't anybody doing anything?" Ben asked, startled.

"The Virginians have sent an officer named George Washington out there to ward them off. But he was driven back. The Indians are joining up with the French. It means war."

The French, who controlled Canada, had been moving down into the Ohio Valley for years. They were hoping to occupy this territory and keep the English from moving inland. France and England were at war with each other in Europe, and now the conflict was breaking out in America.

The English outnumbered the French twenty to one in North America, but the French were better able to maneuver in deep woods. Like the native tribes they traded with, they knew how to put on bear grease in summer to keep insects off. They had learned to blaze trails in the forest, and to travel lightly with very little gear. They made allies of the Indian tribes who worried about the English settlers.

"The French act as one," Ben noted. "But with us, each colony has its own idea about how to operate. We need more unity."

To illustrate his point, Ben published in the *Gazette* a drawing of a snake cut into eight sections, representing the colonies. The caption read, "Join or Die." This was the first American political cartoon.

To put his plan into action, Ben traveled to Albany, New York for a conference of representatives from all the colonies. Albany was an important outpost—the gateway to Canada and to the West.

Many of the delegates were concerned about the threat of the French and Indian War. They had already traded gifts with the Iroquois in exchange for land.

Ben was seeking a more lasting union of the

Ben Warned the General.

colonies. He knew they needed to unite to deal not only with the French threat, but Indian affairs, trade, and land purchases. He was able to convince the delegates to vote in favor of his Albany Plan of Union. It was the first effort to form a single nation from the American colonies. But the individual colonies rejected Ben's plan. Each was afraid to give up any power.

The French and Indians continued to threaten the western part of Pennsylvania. The French established Fort Duquesne at a key river junction, where the city of Pittsburgh is today. They blocked all access to the Ohio Valley.

The English government finally acted. In 1755 General Braddock, the commander of the English forces in America, organized an expedition to take Fort Duquesne. Ben warned the general to be careful.

"You're used to fighting in Europe where the

fields are open," he said. "America is a different place. The French and Indians can be dangerous foes. They know the woods."

"Maybe for your colonial militia that's true," General Braddock answered. "But these are his majesty's troops. We'll easily defeat the savages."

General Braddock was having trouble raising supplies and wagons for his forces. Ben helped, rounding up a great many covered wagons, called Conestoga wagons, and enough supplies to outfit the expedition.

Ben's son William went with General Braddock's army when they set out toward the west. The roads were so bad that the troops were spread out over a long distance. They marched west through the forest for days, finally coming within a few miles of the fort. But there, at the Monongahela River, the French and Indian fighters ambushed them from all sides. The English troops weren't able to group into

A Great Many Wagons

their usual formations in this unfamiliar territory. They fought back, but were defeated. General Braddock was killed.

Messengers came back to Philadelphia with the bad news. Now there was nothing to stop the Indians from sweeping through Pennsylvania.

In December word came to Philadelphia that the Shawnees were raiding in parts of Pennsylvania less than a hundred miles away. Something had to be done.

"We'll form a militia and go up to help the people there," Ben declared. He and William organized 150 horsemen and some supply wagons. They rode off into the dark, cold woods.

In Easton, Pennsylvania, they helped the settlers organize defenses. As they moved farther west, they encountered settlers who were fleeing.

They came to small settlements that had been attacked. The Shawnees had killed people, and even scalped them. They burned the settlers' houses, destroying whole towns.

"We've reached a settlement in Moravian country," Ben wrote to Debby, who was helping by sending supplies to the militia. The Moravians were a group of settlers in the area. "We are building a sturdy stockade to defend against further attacks."

Life was hard out on the frontier. The men had to sleep on the ground. They were wet and cold much of the time. Ben, who was fifty years old, stood up to the difficulties very well. He was still very strong and youthful, with long auburn hair and a broad face.

Ben directed the militiamen to cut down trees and place the logs in a circle to form a stockade. He remembered back when he was a boy, he had played at building forts with his friends. Just as he'd taken charge then, he was the leader now. When the militia returned to Philadelphia, they elected Ben their colonel.

She Was Afraid to Sail.

But Ben lost the election for the Pennsylvania Assembly. The Penn brothers and their allies in America had conspired to punish Ben, even though he was helping to protect their holdings. Ben kept insisting that these rich men help pay for the cost of defense.

"Ben Franklin is a dangerous man," Thomas Penn declared.

The Assembly decided that Ben would be the perfect representative to send to England to negotiate with the Penns over the issue of taxes and rights.

"If my government feels I will be useful, I will go," Ben said.

He pleaded with Deborah to accompany him to England, but she was afraid to sail. She'd never been out of Philadelphia and wasn't about to start traveling now.

So Ben set sail for England to serve the people of his state.

Chapter 13

Life in London

The last time he'd sailed to England, Ben had been a nineteen-year-old boy still learning the printer's trade. Now he was 52, successful, retired from his business, traveling as the representative of all the people of Pennsylvania.

Crossing the ocean was not much safer than it had been thirty years earlier. Sailing ships were still at the mercy of storms and huge waves on the Atlantic. Deborah's fears were justified. Crossing meant two months on a small, heaving ship.

Two Months on a Small, Heaving Ship

BEN FRANKLIN

Approaching the English coast at night, Ben's ship was caught in a gale. It pitched and rolled as the big swells lifted it and let it drop. Luckily, a lookout was able to spot a lighthouse. The captain turned the ship away from the rocks just in time.

"That lighthouse may have saved our lives," Ben noted to his son William who was traveling with him. "When we return to America we should do something about building more lighthouses along the coast. It would be a great benefit for shipping."

William was 26 at the time. When he was fifteen he had tried to run away from home, just as Ben had done. He had wanted to become a pirate. Now he was planning to study law in England. He and Ben were close companions, more like brothers than like father and son.

When they arrived in London, they took rooms in the house of Mrs. Margaret Stevenson and her daughter Polly. This would become their home away from home for a long time. Mrs. Stevenson took good care of Ben. Polly was like another daughter to him and would remain his friend for many years. Unlike most women of the time, she took a keen interest in science and discussed Ben's experiments with him.

London was the biggest city in Europe. Ben found it an exciting place. He set up his electrical apparatus in his room and invited those who were interested to come and see him demonstrate his discoveries.

"This iron ball is charged negatively," he would explain. "Notice what happens when I suspend this cork on a thread, charge that negatively, and bring it near the ball."

The visitors were amazed at the invisible force that made the cork swing away from the ball and float in the air. Ben told them what he had found out about the theories of electrical attraction and repulsion.

He Went to Plays and Concerts.

BEN FRANKLIN

Ben was soon meeting regularly with many interesting thinkers and scientists in London. He went to plays and concerts. He visited the taverns and coffeehouses where the latest ideas were talked about, everything from science to politics. Philadelphia seemed like a small town compared to the mighty city of London.

"The first thing we must do," Ben told William, "is to send gifts back for your mother and sister Sally. I'm sure they're lonely at home without us. There are so many things here that they can't buy in Philadelphia."

Ben asked Mrs. Stevenson and Polly to help pick out gifts. They chose beautiful glass crystal, silk dresses, a satin cloak. Ben bought Deborah a prayer book set in large type so that she wouldn't have to wear her glasses in church.

While Mrs. Stevenson picked out a new carpet for the Franklin home, Ben chose another gift.

"What is that?" Mrs. Stevenson asked him.

"It's a new device for removing the cores from apples," Ben said, always practical. "Debby will love it."

Ben had changed since the old days when he counted every penny. He had plenty of money now and was happy to spend it to make others happy. He even bought himself an embroidered coat and shoes with silver buckles.

Ben had work to do as well. He went to confer with Thomas Penn, who was known as the "Proprietor" of Pennsylvania. Ben presented the opinion of the Pennsylvania Assembly—that the Penn family should pay taxes on their land.

"Those who can afford to should help pay for the well-being of the colony," he insisted. "Farmers and craftsmen who are barely making enough to feed their families can't continue to bear such burdens. The elected representatives in the Assembly

Penn Laughed Out Loud.

have the right to tax and regulate the affairs of the colony."

"Right?" Penn said. He laughed out loud. "What right? King George is the only one with the right to legislate for the colonies. His majesty has given us the power to rule. If people don't want to do as we say, they never should have gone to Pennsylvania."

Ben mentioned that Thomas Penn's father, William, had set up the colony as a "holy experiment." He had established the city as a place of "brotherly love." Penn laughed again. To him, Pennsylvania was a business enterprise. His goal was to make profits for himself, not cater to a crowd of ignorant colonists.

Ben was insulted by Penn's arrogance. But he didn't answer back angrily. He presented the Assembly's petition, which listed all the changes they wanted the Penn family to agree to. Penn barely glanced at the document. He said he would send it to the English attorney–general for an opinion. He didn't contact Ben for another year after that.

"You should really send another representative," he wrote to the Assembly. "This man Franklin is completely unsuitable."

The Assembly supported Ben. They knew that he was trying to negotiate in difficult circumstances. Many wealthy Englishmen sided with the Penns. They didn't like to see the colonies assert claims that they had any rights.

Ben passed the time with music. He learned to play the harp, the guitar and the violin. He went to recitals or sat in on musical evenings in the homes of the many friends he was making in England. He bought a harpsichord and shipped it to America so that Sally could learn to play.

Many of the English people wanted to talk to Ben about what life was like in America. He was the

The Familiar Smell of Printer's Ink

unofficial representative of the colonies in Britain. He liked to explain how strong, self-governing colonies could contribute to the power and glory of the British Empire.

One visit that gave Ben pleasure was going around to the printing house where he'd worked so many years earlier.

"Here's the 'Water-American' come back," said one of the old workers. "He's surely made his fortune in America, he has."

Ben breathed the familiar smell of printer's ink. They were still using the old press he'd operated all those years before. He couldn't help giving one of the young apprentices some words of advice on how to make a clear impression. Knowing how the printer's helpers loved beer, he bought a round for everyone in the shop.

Ben and William traveled north to Ecton, the town where Ben's father had come from. They found the old Franklin farm—the house was now being used as a school. They visited the forge where many generations of Franklins had been blacksmiths. They were able to locate a few distant cousins and exchange family information.

Ben traveled to Scotland, where educated people had long followed his scientific work. At St. Andrew's University he was given an honorary doctor's degree. Oxford University also honored him. After that, he liked to be known as "Doctor Franklin." He was proud of achieving such honors, especially since he had had only two years of formal schooling.

It took three years for Ben to complete negotiations with the Penn family. The outcome was not entirely to his liking, but he did the best he could for Pennsylvania.

He didn't return to America right away. He had grown to like living in England. There were so many

An Honorary Degree

intelligent, well-informed people. Every night he would go out to dinner with friends and engage in lively discussions. Life at the Stevensons' home suited him. He received regular letters from Deborah keeping him posted on all the news back home.

He stayed another two years in London, until 1762. William finished his law studies and became a lawyer in the English courts. In 1761 Ben and William both joined in the celebration of the coronation of King George III.

By that time, William had a son of his own. This baby was named William Temple Franklin, but would always be known as Temple. Who his mother was isn't known. Ben took in his first grandson and helped to take care of him.

The next year, Ben was able to use his contacts to get William a very important position. He was named by the king to be the royal governor of the colony of New Jersey. William married and prepared to go back to America to take up his post.

Ben decided it was time for him to return as well. But he went reluctantly. Both father and son had grown to love England and to think of it as home.

Return to Pennsylvania

Chapter 14

Leadership

Ben had been in England for almost six years before he returned to Pennsylvania in 1762. He was glad to reach home and see Deborah and Sally again.

A year later, England signed a treaty with France that officially ended the French and Indian War. The terms of the treaty put all of America east of the Mississippi River under British control.

Ben wasn't content to stay in Philadelphia and do nothing.

"It's been too long since I've looked after my duties as postmaster general," he told Debby. "I'm going to go out to see how the mail is being delivered. I want you and Sally to come with me."

"I guess I'm a homebody. I just don't like the idea of traveling," Debby said. "I'm happy right where I am."

"Well, *I'm* not a homebody," Sally stated. "I want to go!"

So Ben and his daughter started out to travel up and down the colonies. Their first stop was to visit William and his wife, who now lived in the governor's mansion in Burlington, New Jersey—the same town where Ben as a boy had caught the boat that had first brought him to Philadelphia.

"There are too many people talking against his majesty's government," William said. "Citizens of the colonies should be more loyal."

"The government should answer to the needs of

"I'm Not a Homebody. I Want to Go!"

the people," Ben replied. "You know that a lot of the king's ministers don't really understand us Americans."

The two men discussed the question long into the night.

Ben and Sally moved on, Ben in a two-wheeled carriage, Sally riding on horseback. They travelled along the roads by which the mail went, stopping in many inns along the coast. At each small town they were honored guests. It was a great adventure for Sally, who was nineteen at the time.

In Boston, Ben stayed with his sister Jane Mecom, the only one of all his brothers and sisters still alive. They found Sally a room with one of her Boston cousins. Ben took Sally around to see the house where he had grown up, and the places where he used to play and swim as a boy.

They stayed in Boston all summer. When they returned to Philadelphia after a seven-month trip, they had covered more than 1800 miles. All along the way Ben took steps to improve the delivery of mail. He also met with people and talked to them about conditions in the country.

"They're ordering people out of the western lands," a man in Boston complained. "It's not right."

"I agree," Ben said. "But you know the English government is in debt since our conflict with the French. If people go west, they will be threatened by the Indians. The government in England feels they can't afford to defend us."

"I'll tell you, Ben Franklin," the man answered. "People are getting tired of these English lords deciding what's right for us. We don't even have our own representatives in Parliament."

Just when the colonists thought that peace had arrived on the continent, a new war broke out. Pontiac, chief of the Ottawas, led a rebellion against the English, saying they were building too many forts

The British Had No Mercy.

on tribal lands. The warriors under Pontiac's command captured some of the English forts and killed or drove out many settlers from western Pennsylvania and other areas.

The British had no mercy on the rebellious tribes. They sent them blankets infected with smallpox, hoping to spread the disease among them. The war was brutal on both sides.

Some settlers in Pennsylvania went even further. They attacked peaceful Indians and killed six of them. Two weeks later they raided a workhouse and killed fourteen more Indian men, women and children. English troops stood by and did nothing. The idea of killing all Indians, friend or enemy, was spreading.

The Pennsylvania Assembly ordered the arrest of these murderers, who were known as the Paxton Boys. One hundred forty friendly Indians were then given protection near Philadelphia.

BEN FRANKLIN

The Paxton Boys grew into a mob of more than 300 men. They decided to march into Philadelphia and kill all the Indians, as well as some prominent Quakers, who had always been friendly to Native Americans.

It was midnight when the governor of Pennsylvania came pounding on the door of Ben's house.

"A mob is descending on the city!" he told Ben. "We need to do something. You have to help, Mr. Franklin!"

Once again Ben took on the role of leader. He thought it a little funny, because this governor was the nephew of those same Penn brothers who had opposed him so strongly in England.

Ben organized several hundred militiamen and rounded up some cannon and horses. But rather than fight right away, Ben and three other men rode out to talk to the mob. These frontiersmen had never met a talker like Ben Franklin. He was able

"You Have to Help, Mr. Franklin!"

to convince them to go back to their homes and leave the native people alone.

"Within four and twenty hours," he wrote to a friend in England, "your old friend was a common soldier, a councillor, a kind of dictator, an ambassador to a country mob, and, on his returning home, nobody again."

Later Ben wrote a pamphlet condemning the acts of the Paxton Boys. "What had little boys and girls done," he asked, "that they too must be shot and hatcheted?"

Though Ben had helped Governor Penn out of a difficult situation, the Penn family was far from grateful. A bitter dispute broke out between them and the people's representatives in the Assembly. Ben lost faith that the Penns would ever treat the. colony fairly.

"They are mean, selfish, mercenary men," he declared. He noted with disgust that the governor was offering a reward for the scalps of Indians.

"What's the solution?" his fellow members of the Assembly asked.

"To take the colony away from the Penn family altogether," Ben said. "The king should take over Pennsylvania and stop letting these men dictate to us."

The Penns and their allies waged a brutal election campaign to have Ben removed from the Assembly. They accused Ben of being from the lower classes, of wasting money, taking bribes, anything they could think of. His disapproval of the Paxton Boys cost him the support of some of the frontiersmen who hated Indians. Ben lost the election.

But his party still controlled the Assembly. They voted to send Ben back to England. This time he would ask the king to remove the Penn family as proprietors of the colony.

Ben had only been home for two years. He was

His Supporters Escorted Him to His Ship.

willing to return to London, but he wanted Deborah to come with him.

"You'll love London," he told her. "You'll be able to see plays and hear wonderful music. I want you to meet all the friends I've made there."

But Debby still didn't want to make such a journey. "I was born in Philadelphia," she said, "and this is where I intend to stay."

So Ben had to go off alone. More than 300 of his supporters escorted him to his ship. He intended to stay in England only a few months, long enough to present his petition to his majesty's government. When he boarded the ship, Ben had no idea that this journey would last almost ten years. When he said good-bye to Deborah, he would never have imagined that he would never see his wife again.

Chapter 15

America's Struggle Starts

Ben's official mission in England was to ask the king to take Pennsylvania away from the Penn family. But he was soon caught up in bigger issues.

In order to pay for the cost of defending the colonies, the English government decided to tax the people living in America. This was the first time that England had imposed taxes directly on the colonies—and the colonists didn't like it.

The most hated tax was called the Stamp Act. The people of the colonies had to pay taxes on their

England Imposed Taxes on the Colonies.

newspapers, magazines, almanacs, even playing cards and marriage licenses. A stamp showed that the tax had been paid.

The colonists, who had no representatives in Parliament, had no say in the decision about the tax. In America, everyone was saying, "Taxation without representation is tyranny."

Citizens were furious. In Boston, a crowd wrecked the homes of the tax collector and the lieutenant governor.

"The subject now is the Stamp Act," Sally wrote to her father. "Nothing else is talked about."

Ben went to work to try to get the Stamp Act repealed. As always, he thought that diplomacy would be more effective than violence. He didn't think people should take the law into their own hands. "A firm loyalty to the crown will always be the wisest course to take," he wrote.

He spoke to the English merchants he knew.

"This isn't in your interest," he told them. "You are going to lose business if the dispute goes on."

People in the colonies had already stopped buying many English products in order to protest the tax. Ben talked to anybody in the government who would listen. He wrote sarcastic letters and drew cartoons making fun of the tax.

But since the Stamp Act was the law, he recommended a friend of his to fill a position as tax collector. Word got out that he was in favor of the Stamp Act, that he was siding with the English government against the colonies.

A mob in Philadelphia, angered by these reports, marched on the Franklin home. Sally had to be sent to stay with William. Deborah was determined not to leave her house. She borrowed a squirrel rifle and a couple of pistols. Barricading her door, she stood guard over the house. She refused to budge when the mob ordered her out. She told the

The Crowd Backed Down.

people they were wrong about her husband. The crowd backed down.

The colonies were in turmoil. Men were banding together in groups called Sons of Liberty to resist the tax. Terrible arguments broke out between the Tories, who were loyal to the king, and Patriots, who believed in the rights of the colonies. The issue went beyond just taxes. The whole future of freedom was at stake.

Nine of the colonies sent representatives to a Congress. They declared that England had no right to tax people in America. They asked Ben, as their representative in England, to take their petition to Parliament.

Ben knew he wasn't a great speaker. Instead of giving a speech, he stood before Parliament and answered questions about the Stamp Act. For four hours he answered every point that was brought up, 174 questions in all. The members of Parliament were impressed by his knowledge, and his arguments. He made them see that the Stamp Act was a mistake. A few months later, they repealed the tax. In America, the people celebrated and declared Benjamin Franklin a hero.

Ben settled down in London, living again in his rooms in Mrs. Stevenson's house. Several other colonies hired him to serve as their representative in England. Ben tried to persuade the English government to treat the colonies fairly. He talked to government ministers, wrote letters and articles, tried to make friends among the powerful people of the country. He kept warning them that the colonies were becoming powerful in their own right.

"America will be a great country someday," he said. "We will be able to shake off any shackles."

But the English government grew ever more opposed to the idea that the colonies had any rights.

In 1767 Ben received word that his daughter

The People Declared Ben Franklin a Hero.

Sally planned to marry a man named Richard Bache, an English merchant. Ben gave Sally a dowry of 500 pounds, and wrote to wish her well. He continued to write to his children when they were adults, offering advice and sometimes sending them money.

One of Ben's friends in England was Bishop Shipley, who had five daughters. The girls loved to listen to the stories Ben told about America. When they heard that he had a new grandson in Philadelphia, a boy also called Benjamin, they gave a birthday party for the baby.

Back in America, the English were imposing taxes on all goods imported into the colonies. Again, the people became angry. They burned ships and jeered at English soldiers in their streets. Some Tories were assaulted with tar and feathers, considered a very serious punishment. Tar and feathers stuck to a person and were hard to remove. The victims were then driven from the town.

BEN FRANKLIN

In March of 1770, a group of the Sons of Liberty was making fun of some English troops guarding the custom house in Boston. The Americans threw snowballs. The soldiers panicked and fired their muskets. Five patriots were killed. This incident became known as the Boston Massacre.

Worried about the spread of violence in the colonies, Parliament soon followed Ben's advice and repealed the import tax. They left only one tax, on tea, as a symbol of their right to do what they wanted in the colonies.

By this time Ben had grown eager to return home. He had now been in England almost ten years. Back in Philadelphia, Debby had been sick for some time. Ben was growing tired of trying to get the English government to listen to reason.

He knew things were heating up in the colonies. He kept urging the patriots to restrain themselves, worried that the English would put the colonies

The Boston Tea Party

under even stricter control.

Ben was scheduled to appear before a group of government ministers, called the Privy Council, to argue for the removal of the governor of Massachusetts. Just before he did so, word reached England that a band of patriots in Boston had raided English ships in Boston harbor, throwing hundreds of cases of tea overboard as a protest against English rule. They had dressed as Indians, but everyone knew they were patriots. This is still known as the Boston Tea Party. The English officials were, not surprisingly, furious.

Ben never got a chance to present his petition to the Privy Council. As soon as he appeared before them, a lawyer began to give a speech accusing Ben of all sorts of underhanded deeds.

"These people have no right to ask for the removal of an officer appointed by his majesty," the man argued. "This Ben Franklin is nothing more than a traitor, a scoundrel, and a scheming rogue."

The speech went on for three hours. Ben stood silent. He showed no emotion as the lawyer attacked him, and English aristocrats laughed and jeered at him.

The petition was rejected. Ben was removed from his position as postmaster of the colonies. He knew that his nine years of trying to work with the English had come to nothing. America no longer had any friends in London.

As punishment for the Boston Tea Party, the English closed the port of Boston. They sent troops to crack down on the rebellious colonists there.

"This government," Ben said, "doesn't appear to have enough sense to govern a herd of swine."

Soon afterward, he received more bad news. That winter, Deborah had died of a stroke.

It was time for Ben to return home. In March of 1775, he set sail once again across the Atlantic.

English Aristocrats Laughed at Him.

Chapter 16

From Colonies to Nation

In April of 1775, while Benjamin Franklin was sailing back from England, General Thomas Gage ordered some English troops to march out of Boston. Their plan was to surprise a group of patriots called the Minutemen. The patriots had stored a supply of guns in nearby Concord. The English planned to seize the armaments and teach these rebellious farmers a lesson.

But a Boston silversmith named Paul Revere and his companions rode out at night to warn the

Minutemen. The Americans left their plows behind, took up their muskets, and blocked the bridge at Lexington, on the road to Concord. At dawn, the red-coated English troops arrived. A tense standoff continued for several minutes. Suddenly, shots rang out. Eight Minutemen were killed. The American Revolution had begun.

All over the colonies, the word went out: *To arms! We must fight for our freedom!*

Ben Franklin was afraid of war. He knew the destruction and hardship it would cause. He knew it would be difficult for the colonies to stand up to the most powerful army and navy in the world.

"Which side are you on, Ben?" people began to ask him, practically as soon as he stepped off the ship in Philadelphia. Many thought that Ben's years in England would make him side with the British. Besides, he was 69 years old. He might have grown conservative in his old age, people thought.

Sally and Her Husband Welcomed Ben.

Sally and her husband welcomed Ben to the family's brick house, which he'd never seen. She had several children now.

"Your mother did a fine job overseeing the construction," he told her. "I'm only sorry we couldn't have spent some time here together."

He traveled next to Burlington to talk with William. "These are serious times, son," he said. "The decisions we make will affect the whole future of this country."

In spite of all Ben's arguments, William could not be shaken from his loyalty to the English king who had appointed him governor.

"We owe much to England," William argued. "That is where our duty lies."

The two men could not agree.

"You choose loyalty to your master," Ben said. "I think independence more honorable than any service."

When he left, Ben knew that he would never be close to his son again.

Word spread quickly through Philadelphia. *Ben Franklin is on the side of the patriots! Dr. Franklin is going to support our cause!*

Much work needed to be done. While volunteer soldiers practiced with guns in the streets of Philadelphia, Ben took up his position as a delegate to the Second Continental Congress. The Congress, which met in Philadelphia, was made up of delegates from the colonies. They were creating policies for the new nation.

Besides forming and equipping an army and navy, the Congress had to organize the defense of a long, vulnerable coastline. They had to negotiate with the native tribes in the west. They had to try to get countries in Europe to support them.

In June of 1775, Congress appointed General George Washington commander of all the forces of

Ben Franklin is on the Side of the Patriots!

the colonies. Ben, who knew Washington from the French and Indian War, approved of the choice.

Soon afterward, just outside of Boston, Washington's soldiers clashed with the British in the Battle of Bunker Hill. Though the patriots had to retreat, many English soldiers were killed. People began to realize that this was a real war.

In the fall, Ben traveled to Massachusetts to confer with General Washington.

"The army needs many things," Washington told him. "Food, uniforms, warm clothing. We especially need more guns and gun powder and bullets."

They talked about the best ways to get supplies and to send them to the army in the field. Back in Philadelphia, Ben urged the American Philosophical Society, the scientific group he'd started from the junto years before, to study the question of how to make gunpowder.

He also took over his old position as postmaster

general. Now the colonies would have to set up their own postal system, independent of England.

Everyone in Philadelphia was talking about a pamphlet called "Common Sense." Thomas Paine, whom Ben had first met in England, wrote this pamphlet. Paine criticized the whole idea of a king who had absolute power. He wrote that the colonies should not just fight for their rights, they should break away from England completely.

Soon the idea of independence was on everybody's mind. The Congress appointed Ben Franklin, John Adams and Thomas Jefferson to put the idea into writing. Jefferson wrote the document. Ben helped to make some of the ideas simpler and clearer. The result was the Declaration of Independence, which stated that the thirteen colonies were no longer attached to England, but formed a whole new nation.

The Congress signed the Declaration on July 4,

The Liberty Bell Rang Out in Celebration.

1776. One member, John Hancock, wrote his name very large "so the king can read it without his spectacles."

The Declaration was read in public on July 8th. The Liberty Bell rang out in celebration. A crowd in Philadelphia pulled down and burned the royal coat of arms shield.

"The king no longer rules here!" the people shouted. "Long live Liberty!"

"We must hang together," said one of the members of Congress.

"Yes," Ben joked, "we must hang together or surely we'll hang separately." In fact, all of the men who signed the Declaration were actually committing treason against the king. They would be caught and hanged if the colonies didn't succeed in winning the war.

Unfortunately, the odds were against them. The English had just landed more than 200 ships at

New York, with 30,000 of their best soldiers. General Washington's men were outnumbered two to one. The English defeated the patriots in the Battle of Long Island. Only a quick retreat from New York prevented Washington's army from being captured.

Ben and some other delegates went to New York to meet with the enemy commander, General Howe. Ben had known the general in England and had even played chess with Lady Howe.

"His majesty's government is willing to pardon you," Howe said. "But you must give up your guns and repeal your Declaration of Independence. Then we can discuss your grievances."

"Under those conditions there's nothing to talk about," Ben told him. "We are independent now. The king must recognize that."

"Don't be foolish, Franklin," Howe replied. "You have no chance. His majesty's troops will crush your rebellion."

Ben Met with General Howe.

"Maybe you're right," Ben answered. "But all my life I have seen that ideas have power—more power, sometimes, than an army."

Word of Ben's stubbornness quickly got back to England. Ben Franklin was talked about as one of the worst of the rebels, a traitor to England.

Ben continued to work for the success of the American Revolution. He wrote to his friends in France to urge them to support the colonies against their old enemy, England. But the French weren't ready to act yet. They first wanted to see how the war would go.

Ben had to live with the knowledge that his son William had remained loyal to the king. William had been arrested and was being held in a prison in Connecticut.

"Nothing has ever hurt me so much," Ben said, "as to find myself deserted in my old age by my only son."

BEN FRANKLIN

His grandson Temple, on the other hand, remained loyal to his grandfather. Ben had helped raise Temple and had brought him back from England with him.

One day, Temple, who was fifteen, was playing with his seven-year-old cousin Benjy, Sally's oldest boy. Their grandfather called them aside and spoke to them in a very serious tone.

"Boys, the Congress has sent me on a mission. I'm going to France to try to convince the French to join us in fighting this terrible war."

"How long will you be gone, Grandpa?" Temple asked.

"I'm not sure. Several years, I suspect. I'm an old man and traveling is hard on me. I could use some help from two young men who aren't afraid of a little danger."

The boys' eyes lit up.

"Do you mean it?" Benjy shouted.

"We'll Be Ready, Grandpa."

"Yes, I want both of you to come along with me."

"When to do we leave?" Temple said, jumping up with excitement.

"Soon. We'll sail secretly. We don't want the English to get word of what we're up to."

"We'll be ready, Grandpa."

That night, neither boy could sleep. Both kept imagining the wonderful adventures that awaited them.

Chapter 17

Mission to France

"I see one!" Benjy shouted.

"You do not," Temple said. "You're always saying you see ships."

"This time I'm sure. Look!"

Temple peered out across the dark blue waves. As their ship came to the top of a swell, he saw a mast and a sail way off in the distance.

"You're right!" he said to Benjy. "We've got to tell Captain Wickes."

They went running back to the ship's helm and

206

"We've Got to Tell Captain Wickes."

pointed the ship out to the captain.

"Thank you, boys," he said. "With two lookouts like you, we won't have to worry about those English frigates." The captain of the speedy sloop *Reprisal* maneuvered away from the other ship until it disappeared below the horizon.

It all seemed like a game to Temple and Benjy. They had outrun two English ships already. In fact, very great danger awaited them if they were ever captured. Their grandfather was now one of the most notorious of the American rebels. It was likely that the English would hang Ben if they got their hands on him. The two boys would probably be locked in prison. But they were too excited to be scared.

They helped the sailors on the ship. They fished. They listened to Ben tell stories about other times he had crossed the ocean and about what it would be like in France.

BEN FRANKLIN

Sometimes the trip was not so pleasant. Terrible storms swept over them, heaving the ship up and down and lashing it with rain. For weeks they had nothing to eat except salt beef and biscuits.

The most exciting part of the trip came just before they landed in France. Captain Wickes chased and captured two English merchant ships. Because America was at war with England, any enemy ship was fair game.

When they reached port in France they still had a seventeen-day journey before they arrived in Paris. All along the way people came out to see the great man, Dr. Benjamin Franklin, pass by. They knew him from his *Poor Richard* almanacs. They knew him as a noted scientist, and that he was the representative of the valiant Americans who were struggling for their freedom.

It was odd that this champion of Liberty should be so popular in France. That country was now

They Moved to a Country Setting.

ruled by Louis XVI and his queen, Marie Antoinette. There was no democracy in France. A few thousand aristocrats ran the country. They paid no taxes but put all the burden on the poor people.

When Ben and the boys reached Paris, they lived in a hotel for a while, then moved to a house on the outskirts of the city, in a place called Passy. Ben liked the fresh air and the pretty country setting.

"Temple," he announced, "you will be staying here and helping me out as my secretary. Benjy, I'm sending you to school in Switzerland."

"But Grandpa, I want to stay with you."

"No, the schools are better there. I want you to be educated in a republic, not in a monarchy like France."

Ben immediately went to work. His job was to get the French to give as much aid as possible to the American cause. This wasn't easy. The colonies had no central government that could promise to repay the aid.

Some Frenchmen were willing to lend the American patriots money and supplies. These were shipped secretly though the West Indies, and then had to pass through the English blockade. Ben knew how desperate General Washington's army was for any supplies.

He wanted to convince the French government to recognize the new American nation, but he knew that the colonies would have to prove themselves on the battlefield first.

The Revolutionary War was not going well. Washington's troops had to retreat from New York. They didn't have enough guns. Many soldiers even lacked shoes. They were forced to march barefoot even in winter. English forces had occupied Philadelphia. They had even taken over Ben's house, forcing Sally and her family to flee. There

The Army Was Desperate for Supplies.

was a rumor that the English General Burgoyne was marching down from Canada to split the colonies in half.

One thing Ben did was to help out a young American named John Paul Jones. Jones was captain of one of the few warships the Americans had on the seas. He captured a British ship and brought it to France. Ben managed to get the French to give Jones a bigger ship with more guns. Jones named it the *Bonhomme Richard*, which was French for "Poor Richard."

Jones then sailed up the coast of England. He sent raiding parties into English harbors to burn ships. Finally he got into a fierce battle with an English warship. The *Bonhomme Richard* was sunk, but Jones's men managed to capture the English ship and sail it back to France.

One afternoon, as Ben was working in his office, Temple came running in, all out of breath.

"Grandpa," he said. "A messenger has just come. He says General Burgoyne has been defeated!"

"Are you sure?" Ben asked.

"Yes. Our men fought the English at a place called Saratoga, north of Albany. They beat them."

"This is good news, Temple," Ben said. "Very good news."

The American militia, farmers who had taken up arms, had defeated the best English troops and stopped their plan to split the colonies. Ben immediately went to work informing important people in France of the victory. Now, he assured them, they could have confidence in the colonies' chances of winning their War of Independence.

The climate changed in France. Wealthy Frenchmen began to send supplies to America openly. Many men applied to Ben to join up and serve in the colonial army.

A Meeting with the French Ruler

Best of all, the French government decided to recognize America as a nation. The victory at Saratoga came in October of 1777. By February of 1778, Ben had negotiated a treaty of alliance with France. Spain and Holland also took up the cause of the colonies. They all wanted to see England defeated.

Ben was granted a meeting with the French ruler. King Louis was a dandy who insisted that everyone around him dress up in silk suits with ruffles and lace trim. When Ben arrived wearing a plain brown suit and without a white powdered wig, they almost didn't allow him in. But the king was friendly to the "backwoodsman." Ben thanked him very sincerely for the help France was giving to the Americans.

While this was happening, Washington's army was spending a freezing winter at Valley Forge, Pennsylvania. Many of the troops were dressed only in rags, and had to wrap their feet in rags as well. No one had enough to eat.

Three more long years of struggle lay ahead for the American forces. Ben continued to work in France to raise money for the army. He bought his own printing press, using his skill as a printer to publish information advancing the American cause. He wrote letters to influential people. He applied his lifetime of practice at convincing and persuading through the written word, his way of helping his country's revolution.

In the summer of 1781, more news reached France. An army of French troops had arrived in America to join with Washington's soldiers. The two forces had managed to trap the English army in Yorktown, Virginia. They defeated the redcoats and forced them to surrender.

Against all odds, with French help, the Americans had defeated Great Britain, the most powerful

He Bought His Own Printing Press.

country in the world. Everyone, from the farmers who had stood their ground at Lexington, to Ben Franklin, who had worked for years to win help for the American side, was proud of the result. The former British colonies were now a free and independent nation.

Chapter 18

Working for Peace

"Where are we going, Grandpa?" Benjy asked.

"We're going to see a man fly," Ben said.

"Aw, you're joking with me," the boy replied.

"Am I? You'll see."

Benjy was visiting his grandfather in Paris during a vacation from school. Ben was teaching him how to operate the printing press he had in his house. Benjy wanted to be a printer when he grew up.

How can a man fly? the boy wondered. *Would*

"Is He Actually Going to Fly?"

he have wings like a bird?

They arrived at a large open field. Thousands of people were gathered there to watch. Benjy caught sight of the biggest balloon he'd ever seen in his life. Under it was hanging a basket large enough for a man to stand in. A flame kept hot air flowing into the bottom of the balloon.

"Is he actually going to fly?" Benjy asked his grandfather.

"We'll soon find out," Ben said.

As they watched, the ropes that tied the balloon down were let loose. The big balloon slowly rose into the air. It kept going up and up until it looked no bigger than an orange. The crowd was amazed. People pointed and cheered. It was the first time in history that a man had left the earth.

"This is silly," a man in the crowd declared. "What good is a balloon, anyway?"

Ben answered, "What good is a newborn baby?

BEN FRANKLIN

No one knows what a person may become. No one knows the possibilities that might develop from any discovery."

Ben continued to live in France after the American Revolution was over. He was now the official minister to France from the new United States of America. Along with John Adams and John Jay, Ben had been asked by Congress to carry out the peace negotiations with England. Congress knew that Ben had life-long experience as a negotiator and peacemaker.

The English were disappointed to have lost their colonies. They were slow to agree to the terms of the peace. They kept trying to split the Americans and the French. But Ben knew how much France had done to help his country win independence. He would only agree to a peace that included all of America's allies.

Ben had become very popular in France. He

The Official Minister of the United States

went around dressed in his plain clothes, wearing a fur hat and carrying a walking stick made from a crabapple limb. He represented the New World: simple, practical, witty. Many portraits were painted of him. His face could be seen on medals, rings, watches and snuff boxes.

"My face is as well known," he wrote to Sally, "as that of the moon." Ben made many friends in Paris. He was especially popular with the ladies, who called him "My dear Papa." He often had dinner with them and afterward played chess or cards. He had so many stories to tell from his long life that everyone was eager to have him visit.

One day at Passy, Ben received a letter from his son William. William had spent two years in prison as a loyalist who wouldn't support the American cause. After his release, he had gone to England to live. Now that the war was over, William was writing to Ben suggesting that they could be friendly again.

But Ben still felt the pain of William's betrayal. He answered the letter. Ben sent Temple over to England to visit his father. But he never invited William to come and see him. They would meet briefly before Ben returned to America, but relations between them remained cool.

In September of 1783, the English agreed to sign a peace treaty. The document said that the colonies would become a free, sovereign, and independent nation.

Ben was ready to go home now. But Congress knew he was a valuable representative. They asked him to establish relations with other nations in Europe. As always, Ben did his duty.

For two more years he helped set up commercial ventures and agreements with various countries. To show the Europeans how a democratic government worked, he printed and circulated

Time for Ben to Return

copies of the constitution he'd helped write for Pennsylvania.

Finally, in the spring of 1785, Congress sent the young Virginian Thomas Jefferson over to replace Ben as minister to France. It was time for Ben to return to Philadelphia.

Though he was homesick, he was also sad to leave. He liked the French people, and he had many friends there. For a week before he left, people threw parties and elaborate farewell ceremonies. He was presented with an image of King Louis surrounded by 408 diamonds.

By this time, Ben was quite ill. He suffered from gout and kidney stones. It was painful for him to ride in a carriage. His friends borrowed a litter that was used by the queen. This was how he traveled to the port—in a chair suspended on poles between two mules.

He boarded the ship that would take him home.

BEN FRANKLIN

He was 79 years old now. Benjamin Franklin had
served his country for many years. He was making
his eighth trip across the Atlantic. He knew it would
be his last.

He Was 79 Years Old Now.

Chapter 19

Ben Franklin, American

"Why are those bells ringing?" someone asked on a street in Philadelphia, one sunny September day in 1785.

"Haven't you heard?" another man answered. "Ben Franklin has come back. His ship is just docking now."

The two men joined all the others rushing to Market Street Wharf.

Ben was amazed as he stepped off the ship that had carried him home from France. Here he was at the same spot where he had first set foot in Philadelphia more than sixty years before. Then, he'd been a runaway printer's apprentice. Now, he was one of the most famous men in the world.

Ben's reception was certainly different than the one he'd experienced as a teenager. Bells were ringing all over town. Cannons fired in his honor. Thousands of people gathered to see him. They shouted and cheered.

"The affectionate welcome I met with from my fellow citizens was far beyond my expectation," Ben would later say.

Sally was there to meet him when he arrived. She had seven children now, and she introduced each of them to their famous grandfather.

The crowd of people, still cheering, accompanied Ben up Market Street to his brick house. Walking along in the sunshine, Ben thought of a morning like this many years before, and of a girl he had seen

Ben Received an Endless Stream of Visitors.

then, sweeping her steps.

"I have so much to tell you, Father," Sally said.

She described how the English troops had occupied Philadelphia. She had had to flee with her husband and children. An English officer took over their house. When he left, he'd stolen many of Ben's musical instruments. "He even took Temple's schoolbooks," she said.

She told about everyone's efforts during the war and how glad they were to receive help from France.

"Everyone's been talking about you," she said. "I think they're going to elect you president of Pennsylvania."

And so they did. Ben served three terms as the president of the Commonwealth of Pennsylvania, which was like being governor.

He received an endless stream of visitors. Members of the American Philosophical Society came to confer with him. All the officers of the Union Fire

Company, which he had started many years before, showed up to welcome him.

"I still have my bucket and equipment," Ben told them. "I'll be ready to answer the alarm." But he was sick now and really could hardly walk.

One of those who came was George Washington, who in a few years would be elected the nation's first president. These two men, who had done the most to win America's independence, became close friends.

Ben planned an addition to his house so that he could have a large library for his many books and scientific devices. During construction he found that one of the lightning rods on his roof was partly melted after being struck by lightning. His own house had been saved by his invention!

Ben spent many hours sitting under a big mulberry tree in his backyard, often playing with his grandchildren. He told them stories about when he

Ben Spent Hours with His Grandchildren.

was a little boy in Boston, about the stone wharf he and his friends had made so that they could catch fish in a pond.

He helped Benjy get established as a printer. Together they published some books for children, which Ben thought would help young people learn to read more quickly. Following in his grandfather's footsteps, Benjy would go on to become a successful newspaper editor.

Things in the new nation were not going well. The states, loosely joined together under the Articles of Confederation, were all going in different directions. Without any central authority there was no way to collect taxes or reach trade agreements with other countries. Something needed to be done.

In 1787 twelve of the states sent delegates to Philadelphia to draw up a new constitution for the country. Ben was one of the delegates from Pennsylvania. He supported George Washington as head of the convention.

During the meetings, which dragged out for four months that summer, Ben did not say much. He was 81 years old. He had to be carried to the convention in a chair.

"I wish I could be lifted into the air by a balloon," he said, "and have a man lead me along on a string."

In spite of his illness, he never missed a single meeting of the Constitutional Convention. He was always ready to suggest a compromise or to urge the delegates to be more tolerant of the views of others.

Though he was ill, Ben continued to write letters and meet with people.

One of the last causes Ben took up was the movement to abolish slavery. Even though he had once owned slaves himself, he now felt that slavery had no place in a country that declared that "all men are created equal."

BEN FRANKLIN

He was named president of the Pennsylvania Society for Promoting the Abolition of Slavery. One of the last letters he ever wrote mocked a congressman for defending slavery. He petitioned Congress not just to free all the slaves but to give them education and an opportunity to earn a living.

On April 17, 1790, with his family gathered at his bedside, Benjamin Franklin died. He was 84 years old.

People all over America and France mourned Ben's death. More than 20,000 people turned out to see him laid to rest, the biggest funeral ever in Philadelphia.

In his long life, Benjamin Franklin had seen a nation born.

Remembering what his father had told him as a boy, he had always tried to be useful. He had never turned his back on his duty. Always he had found happiness in doing good for others.

IGB - IGB / 5923 - 1 / 1716